THE
DECISION-MAKING
POCKETBOOK

By Neil Russell-Jones

Drawings by Phil Hailstone

"In an internet start-up, speed of decision and risk reduction are critical. I found this comprehensive yet clear and simple book a great help in structuring and prioritising decisions."
Michel Sabatier, Director, OpticalServe.com

"An excellent insight into the decision-making process. A pragmatic approach, showing how to ensure management by design rather than chance."
Belinda Moore, General Manager, Thomson Travel

Published by:
Management Pocketbooks Ltd
Laurel House, Station Approach, Alresford, Hants SO24 9JH, U.K.
Tel: +44 (0)1962 735573   Fax: +44 (0)1962 733637
E-mail: sales@pocketbook.co.uk
Website: www.pocketbook.co.uk

This edition published 2000. Reprinted 2002, 2004.

© Neil Russell-Jones 2000.

ISBN 1 870471 76 8

British Library Cataloguing-in-Publication Data – A catalogue record for this book is available from the British Library.

Design, typesetting and graphics by **efex ltd**. Printed in U.K.

CONTENTS

1 INTRODUCTION

CONGRATULATIONS!

Congratulations! You have (probably) made several decisions that have led you to this page:

- To enter a bookshop
- To look in the business section
- To pick up a book on decision-making
- And now you may possibly decide to buy it!

Most of these decisions will have been made subconsciously unless you went out proactively (consciously) with the objective of buying a book on decision-making.

The majority of decisions we make are subconscious, made without deep analysis and often on 'auto-pilot' - but always affected by a wide range of factors depending on the situation. In a typical morning, we will make decisions about what clothes to wear, what to have for breakfast, how to get to work, etc.

At work we make another set of decisions - some work-related, some personal. Certainly, work-related decisions will be taken within a set formulaic manner, whether formal or informal, that allows us to influence the outcome in some way.

HOW THIS BOOK IS STRUCTURED

This book is about decision-making - or **how** to decide between choices.

It is structured into two parts:

- The first part (chapters 1 and 2) consists of an **introduction**, with a definition of what a decision actually is, and a **framework** for taking and making decisions

- Part two (chapters 3 to 6) explores the **substance** behind the framework and considers group dynamics, methodologies and tools, how to communicate a decision, and concludes with some tips

WHAT IS A DECISION?

What it is - According to the dictionary, the verb 'decide' means 'to determine, to end, to resolve, to settle and to make up one's mind', while the noun 'decision' is 'the act of settling, making up one's mind', etc. Someone in a position of power is said to be a 'decision-maker' and we refer to those who do make up their mind as 'resolute' or 'decisive'.

The Latin root of the word means to 'cut away'. This points to **what a decision really is:** to cut away the surrounding clutter, to enable one to see a path to an objective and, by taking a decision (or a series of decisions), to follow that path with all of its implications.

What it is not - A decision is not allowing events to take their course willy-nilly. If you did, an outcome would still occur - but one not influenced or decided upon with due regard to the surrounding circumstances. Such an outcome represents an inability or lack of desire to analyse and reach a conclusion; control has been surrendered. This might not matter - for example, when merely choosing what perfume to wear - but can be of major consequence where commercial or other vital decisions are required.

WHAT IS A DECISION?

'To be, or not to be, that is the question' (Hamlet)

Decision-making is about **deliberately opting** for one choice from two or more, **proactively** to optimise a situation or outcome and not let it happen by default.

It is also about trying to minimise the element of chance or risk in life, by taking decisions and actions that will influence the outcome in one's favour.

To sum up, decision-making is:

- The selection of an option over others (which could include no action)
- Under conditions that are uncertain
- Which exposes you to a risk
- In order to reach a specified goal, objective or outcome.

There must be a choice and it must be taken proactively, otherwise it is merely an occurrence.

5

KEY COMPONENTS

The process involves getting from an identified need to a decision that addresses the need and the real issues. At the same time it is necessary to minimise the risks of the issues and the consequences of the decision.

WHY SOME DECISIONS ARE HARDER THAN OTHERS

While some decisions are easy (what to eat for supper) many more are extremely hard. Usually, a hard decision involves greater consequences/implications or, in some cases, a higher level of resource commitment.

In reality, not all so-called hard decisions are hard. Some feel harder than others owing to scale:

- If a friend asks to borrow £5 you're likely to oblige without thinking about it

- If that friend asks to borrow £1,000 you're likely to be circumspect and ask questions

The decision is the same one in essence - concerning creditworthiness. But, where the amount is greater, we perceive the decision to be much harder because the consequences are greater. Who cares about £5? But, £1,000 is a sum most people would not wish to lose. It represents a risk, but at what stage does the decision become hard - £6, £25, more? The risk is that the friend might not or cannot repay the money and, therefore, you might regret your decision. Your decision will be based on your consideration of the risk and the magnitude of the possible loss, although you might not see it in this way.

DEFINING HARD DECISIONS

We can define a decision as having 'hard' characteristics when:

- **The situation is uncertain** - ie: there is a greater perceived risk

And also when:

- **The situation is inherently complex with many different issues** - eg: the siting of a new airport is immensely complex, especially in these environmentally-aware times, because of the factors that must be taken into consideration (flight paths, air traffic control, slots, residents, communications links, etc)
- **There are several objectives but one or more is blocked** and compromises or trade-offs are needed
- **Different perspectives can lead to different conclusions** - especially true where two or more people are involved in making a decision; they may disagree about the assumptions, probable outcomes or, even, the decision

The key issue is how to handle hard decisions to ensure they are taken as painlessly as possible. This requires the use of a robust, consistent approach and an appropriate level of detail - essential to ensure that risk is minimised or, at least, understood.

BENEFITS OF THE RIGHT APPROACH

A robust, consistent approach to decision-making, together with the required supporting analysis, will:

- Deal with the **complexities** by providing a structure within which the issues can be organised (human beings have real problems dealing with five or more variables)

- Identify **uncertainty** and then present this in a structured and helpful manner

- Deal with a multiplicity of **objectives and trade-offs**

- Analyse different perspectives and facilitate logical presentation, in order to **obtain consensus/decisions,** especially where several opinions are present

- Encourage **flexibility** to change as circumstances alter and which may invalidate or fundamentally alter the appropriateness of the decision

- Provide an **'audit trail'** demonstrating how the decision was reached, what was considered, who was involved, etc (very useful when things go wrong and 'regret' is considered)

SOME DECISION-MAKING ERRORS

Research has identified a few very common errors or points to watch out for when making decisions, in particular:

- **Haste** - not to be confused with speed. A decision is made before the facts are available or without taking the facts into account. *Decide in haste - regret at leisure.*
- **Narrow perspective** - often results in addressing the wrong issue because the real issue has been pre-judged or confined within a framework of analysis that is inappropriate.
- **Over-confidence** - either in the decision itself or, more commonly, in the understanding of the issue and facts.
- **Rules-of-thumb** - relying on rough frameworks or shortcuts for important decisions instead of carrying out adequate analysis.
- **Filtering** - screening out unpleasant findings or those that do not support pre-conceived notions or the decision you want to make.
- **Juggling** - lack of analytical framework and, therefore, trying to manage many variables or pieces of information in your head.

A proper framework helps obviate these problems.

A FRAMEWORK FOR
DECISION-MAKING

A FRAMEWORK FOR DECISION-MAKING

SEVEN KEY STEPS

There are seven key steps to decision-making:

1 **Define** correctly the real decision to be made
2 **Understand** the context in which the decision needs to be made
3 **Identify** the options
4 **Evaluate** the consequences of each option
5 **Prioritise** the options and choose one
6 **Review** the decision taken (possible re-work)
7 **Take action** to effect the decision

Unless step 7 is taken then no real decision has been made and it has been an exercise in futility.

You must, of course, live with the consequences of the decision. If, however, you have followed a logical process, as outlined above, then you would expect these to be within your tolerances.

A FRAMEWORK FOR DECISION-MAKING

SEVEN KEY STEPS

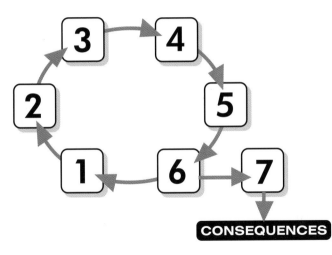

A FRAMEWORK FOR DECISION-MAKING

PROTO-DECISION-MAKING QUESTIONS

Before starting to make a decision it is necessary to think through a few points to place the decision in context and frame the process:

- How should this decision be made - what is the most appropriate forum or mechanism:
  - Solely?
  - In groups?
  - Who should be involved?

- Has it been made before - if so, what were the outcomes or lessons?

- Does it affect other decisions - if so, how?

- Does it need to be taken at all - is it redundant?

- What is the urgency/timing - when does it need to be made?

- To get a different perspective, consider how someone else would handle it. For example, in a business context how would your main competitor handle the issue?

- Where should the greater emphasis be placed in the process (data gathering, analysis, consultation, communication, etc)?

1. DEFINE THE DECISION

This is the first step and also the most critical.

Whereas some decisions undoubtedly turn out incorrect, because they are based on poor analysis, most decisions 'go wrong' because the wrong issue requiring a decision is identified - the symptoms rather than the true causes are addressed.

Thus, the first step involves analysis of the real drivers of the situation and identification of the true issues that the decision must address. The key questions here are:

- Why am I making this decision - what is my aim or objective in making it?

- What has led to the situation that now demands a decision and what does it really require?

1. DEFINE THE DECISION

EXAMPLE

In visiting a company and seeing piles of files stacked up high and people overworked, it would be easy to assume from a *superficial initial analysis* that filing was an issue and to decide to purchase more filing cupboards and, perhaps, take on extra filing staff.

A better and deeper understanding based on *causal analysis* would indicate that there is a problem with the process itself, which is fragmented and very inefficient. The result is slow throughput times and long delays.

Detailed analysis of the real cause, possibly by process re-engineering, would obviate the need to buy filing cabinets and, more importantly, benefit both staff and customers.

Superficial question	'How do I improve my filing?'
Real question	'What must I do to improve the management of paper?' (ie: the process)

1. DEFINE THE DECISION

OBJECTIVES: FUNDAMENTAL vs MEANS

It is important to understand the difference between **fundamental** objectives and **subsidiary** objectives (often called **means** objectives) - things you must achieve on the way to your fundamental objectives.

For example, a personal objective might be to enjoy a very good lifestyle later on in life. This could be supported by subsidiary objectives:

- obtain adequate qualifications
- find a well-paid job
- buy a ski chalet
- build a good pension fund
- retire at 55
- etc.

It is vital that fundamental objectives be used to drive the decision-making process. Subsidiary objectives should only be considered when they enhance achievement of the fundamental objective.

A FRAMEWORK FOR DECISION-MAKING

1. DEFINE THE DECISION

QUESTIONS TO CLARIFY YOUR MOTIVES

Ask yourself:
- Is the objective clear?
- Have all options been identified?
- Has data been gathered to support the analysis?
- Has the analysis been carried out and a brief prepared? The brief should explain:
  - the impact from each option
  - the risk of the option
  - the likelihood of the risk occurring
  - the cost of doing it
  - the implications of not doing it
  - timing

Unless you have the answers to these questions then you will not be clear as to why you are making the decision. Therefore, you cannot hope to make the right one, nor to understand the real drivers of the need to make the decision.

2. UNDERSTAND THE CONTEXT

Context is crucial to understanding the real nature of
the decision to be made and the needs it addresses.
It's impossible to take decisions in isolation from the situation;
you cannot disregard the circumstances or context. Doing so will not,
of course, preclude you from making a decision but it will be the wrong one or,
at least, sub-optimal (unless you're lucky).

For example, the same set of facts when presented in support of a strategy will exert
different influences on a decision depending on the operational sector and the particular
market within that sector. For a global oil company the situation in, say, the UK market will
play a minor part in setting strategy. However, a food retailer operating wholly within a
market will take the trends therein and the likely outcomes very seriously.

A bank, for instance, deciding on the future of its network cannot ignore the probability of
demographic changes that will alter customer profiles and demands for its products. Nor
can technology be ignored: with the increasing penetration of e-mail and voice mail, the net
present value of a branch network may be negative and, therefore, require major changes
to the bank's strategy.

2. UNDERSTAND THE CONTEXT

ACTION	*is preceded by*	PLANNING
PLANNING	*is preceded by*	DECISION
DECISION	*is preceded by*	RISK ANALYSIS
RISK ANALYSIS	*is preceded by*	DECISION NEED RECOGNITION
DECISION NEED RECOGNITION	*arises from the*	CONTEXT

Therefore, you always begin with the CONTEXT which (in totality) is always unique.

A FRAMEWORK FOR DECISION-MAKING

2. UNDERSTAND THE CONTEXT

EACH SITUATION IS UNIQUE

You cannot take a decision in a given situation and then assume every subsequent decision will fall within the same parameters.

Even in a small, well-defined set of circumstances there will be gradual, almost imperceptible, changes in the situation that need to be recognised and factored into the ultimate decision. In a larger, more complex set of circumstances - such as the whole of the USA or the Euroland economy - the circumstances within which you are operating will change every day and for each decision within this context the impact of these changes needs to be understood.

Example: For a major international player the decision on where to take profits or locate an operation will, in part, be driven by the prevailing tax regimes. When the regime changes then not only must the effect of this particular change be understood but also the comparative effect needs to be examined. This is because a relative advantage may no longer pertain and a substantial shift in thinking may be necessary. This could well result in a major strategic evaluation. For example, if a withholding tax on eurobonds was introduced into the UK, then much of the business would shift elsewhere with enormous consequences for the UK financial markets. Would the big trading houses still need such a large centre of operations in London?

2. UNDERSTAND THE CONTEXT

EXAMPLE

The decision on where to buy a house may be changed for various reasons. There might be a sudden election of a new, local government committed to higher property charges. Alternatively, plans may be put forward to build a new superstore or motorway near the house, hence the need to carry out a search prior to buying.

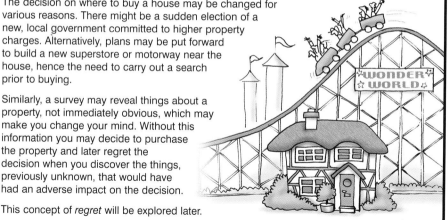

Similarly, a survey may reveal things about a property, not immediately obvious, which may make you change your mind. Without this information you may decide to purchase the property and later regret the decision when you discover the things, previously unknown, that would have had an adverse impact on the decision.

This concept of *regret* will be explored later.

2. UNDERSTAND THE CONTEXT

ANALYSIS

Analysis of the situation is critical. This involves a real understanding of:

- The situation:
  - What is the ambit of the issue?
  - What has been done previously and what worked?

- The factors that will influence the situation. For example, in a business context:
  - Who are the major players?
  - What are the buying behaviours?
  - What is the impact of technology?
  - What are the demographic issues?
  - What are the competing products?
  - What are the substitutes?

- What the impact of these factors will be - usually in a range of outcomes as the future is uncertain and is more easily understood in a range. People prefer to see comparatives as they allow a greater understanding of the differences between items and provide a framework within which it is easier (or more comfortable) to operate.

- What the key or critical success factors will be in the given situation.

- Who will be impacted by the decision.

- Who needs to be involved in the decision and in what way (their roles).

2. UNDERSTAND THE CONTEXT

INFORMATION vs DATA

Analysis must be based on *information* not *data.*

A list detailing the ages of every householder in a given locale over the last 10 years is *data* not *information*.

An analysis of the changes that have taken place in those households over time - the trends - is, however, *information* not *data*. It allows an understanding of the context or situation and can form a valuable input into, for example, decisions on how to market services to the householders.

Remember **DRIP** when analysing:

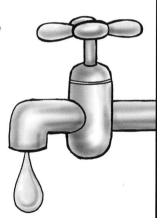

Data Rich, Information Poor

Volume does not equal quality.

2. UNDERSTAND THE CONTEXT

STRIKING A BALANCE

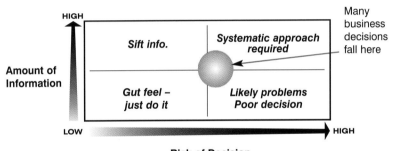

To enable you to analyse the risks, you must strike a balance between the **risk of the decision** and the **amount of information** you have.

2. UNDERSTAND THE CONTEXT

KNOWLEDGE IS POWER

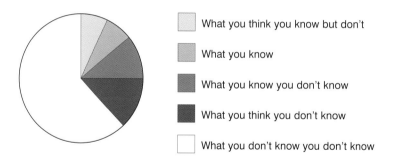

What you think you know but don't

What you know

What you know you don't know

What you think you don't know

What you don't know you don't know

- **What you know is a lot less than you think**
- You must have the right level of information to make an informed decision

3. IDENTIFY THE OPTIONS

A major difficulty often cited in decision-making is
the lack of options, especially when none of the options
seems to address the real needs. This is usually the result of
inadequate analysis that has not identified the proper situation and
what might be done to address the issues. Lack of *creativity* is another reason.

Generating sufficient options, particularly in complex situations requiring imaginative solutions, is a great challenge. It is often useful to spend time considering a wide range of options - wider even than during the initial thinking phase. There are several ways of doing this:

- Brainstorming - where ideas are collected without criticism and then considered.

- Bringing in diverse groups of people with different perspectives and experience. Example: an organisation had a problem with its lifts; people were complaining that they were slow, noisy, etc. The team assembled included unusual members such as psychologists, who recommended that mirrors be installed, and complaints ceased.

- Using things out of context. Example: in a brick factory, using trigger cards with off-the-wall objects not normally considered as brick-like (eg: pomegranates, fish or kangaroos) and developing ideas from that.

3. IDENTIFY THE OPTIONS

ANALYSIS vs COMPLEXITY

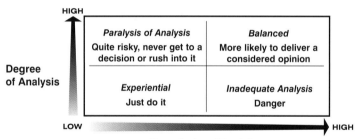

Degree of Analysis

HIGH

Paralysis of Analysis **Quite risky, never get to a decision or rush into it**	*Balanced* **More likely to deliver a considered opinion**
Experiential **Just do it**	*Inadequate Analysis* **Danger**

LOW   HIGH

Complexity of Decision

It is important to undertake the right level of analysis, according to the complexity of the decision.

Remember, it is only necessary to carry out *adequate analysis* to enable you to take the decision - the incremental benefits from any more than this are not worth the effort.

3. IDENTIFY THE OPTIONS

OVER-ANALYSIS

Paralysis of analysis slows down decision-making and can also reduce its effectiveness.

Too much data clouds perspective and leads to errors unless handled properly. Moreover, as the amount of *evidence* increases, so confidence in the (less accurate) decision also increases (piles of data give a warm feeling). This leads to over-confidence in the decision and poor decision-making.

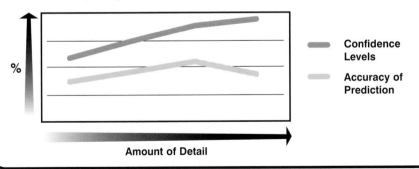

Confidence Levels

Accuracy of Prediction

%

Amount of Detail

4. EVALUATE THE CONSEQUENCES

Decision-making is **not** about whether *to take a risk or not.* It **is** about how to *take reasonable risks* and how to evaluate the *impact* of those risks. Reasonableness is, of course, subjective and differs between people, organisations and situations.

What it really boils down to is…
Which option has the most acceptable set of consequences, given my current context and my desired goals?

This means understanding the true consequences of the decision and also brings in the concept of regret…
What will be my level of regret if I do this and what will it be if I don't?

In essence, we are talking here about the potential negative value placed on the consequences of the action (or inaction).

4. EVALUATE THE CONSEQUENCES

THE ROLE OF ANALYSIS

Analysis provides input to a decision and should only be undertaken to support a point. It might be carried out to enable a series of options to be thrown into greater clarity or contrast, or it might enable options to be developed.

There are two types of analysis, deductive and inductive. Use the deductive approach as this is far more effective and generally easier to understand.

'When you have eliminated the rest, whatever remains (however unlikely) must be the answer, Watson'.

4. EVALUATE THE CONSEQUENCES

INDUCTIVE vs DEDUCTIVE ANALYSIS

Deduction presents a logical flow of reasoning that leads to a *therefore* conclusion. Example:

- All fish swim and have fins
- I am a fish and have fins
- *Therefore,* I can swim.

Key to this logic is that the second point will comment on the first point.

Induction, however, presents a group of facts or ideas from which a conclusion can be inferred - one that is open to several different interpretations unless the facts are so overwhelming that there is only one conclusion that can be drawn.

For example, the fact that foreign aircraft carriers and soldiers have arrived in a particular locality, and telephones lines are down, could lead one to infer that a war is taking place. But, it could also be a rescue operation after, say, an earthquake. It all depends on the context.

A FRAMEWORK FOR DECISION-MAKING

4. EVALUATE THE CONSEQUENCES
REGRET

This is the analysis of what the decision will mean:
- What will I regret if I do this - or don't do this?
- How much will I regret this?
- When might it happen?
- How might it happen?

Put another way, can I handle the loss that might accrue from taking this course of action? And, what is the probability of it occurring?

You may pose these questions when, for example, planning to:
- Gamble
- Invest in (risky) stocks
- Lend money to someone
- Insure someone or something

4. EVALUATE THE CONSEQUENCES

REGRET

Some key examples of regret not being sufficiently considered:

- Bhopal. The regret of an explosion was insufficiently considered when deciding to site the plant in a populous area. Nor was the possibility of subsequent legal actions in the USA taken into account.

- Non-clean up of toxic sites, resulting in adverse publicity, clean up costs and fines.

- The decision by World War I generals to release gas when the wind was blowing towards their own side!

Consider, for example, a female smoker trying to take the decision to give up cigarettes:

What will she regret if she gives up? Short-term, it could be the pleasurable effects from nicotine inhalation and the physiological and psychological props. What will she regret if she doesn't give up? Long-term, the probability of a severely debilitating illness or disease, general ill-health, possible social shunning as tolerances change, and increased cost of health care.

In reaching her decision she will take these factors into account and decide which is the least regrettable course of action. If she is organised she might display them in tabular form (see opposite) and then 'weight' them according to her views.

A FRAMEWORK FOR DECISION-MAKING

4. EVALUATE THE CONSEQUENCES
REGRET

Tabulation of decision to give up smoking

	Give up	**Don't give up**
Benefits	• Improved cashflow • Improved social acceptance • Cleaner taste buds • No smelly clothes	• Social prop • Physiological prop • Keep weight down
Regrets	• No social prop • No nicotine pleasure • No physiological prop • Pain and anguish	• Severe illness • Reduced social acceptance • Marred taste buds • Smelly clothes

(unweighted)

4. EVALUATE THE CONSEQUENCES

CAUTION vs COURAGE

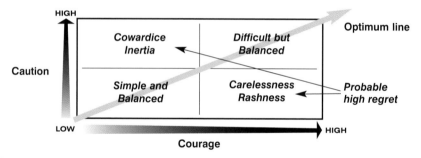

Two opposite forces pull the decision-making:

Courage to take the decision pulls you towards taking the decision (faint heart never won)

Caution of the consequences pulls you towards shirking the decision (fools rush in)

Letting one force dominate will almost certainly lead to a high degree of regret.

A FRAMEWORK FOR DECISION-MAKING

4. EVALUATE THE CONSEQUENCES

RISK ASSESSMENT MATRIX

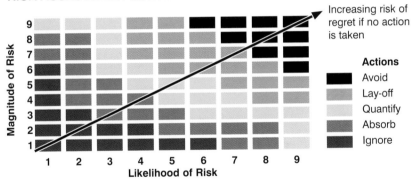

Increasing risk of regret if no action is taken

Actions

Avoid

Lay-off

Quantify

Absorb

Ignore

Risk is an important issue when evaluating the consequences of a decision. How risky is this *thing* and what is the probability of it occurring (in the given context)? This grid allows you to understand these two criteria by placing a weighting on the issues and plotting the criteria. Action can then be decided accordingly.

4. EVALUATE THE CONSEQUENCES
EXPECTED VALUE ANALYSIS

'Expected Value' (EV) is a system for analysing regret arithmetically. EV is the measure of the gain (or loss) from a decision, derived by multiplying the probability of an outcome by the value of that outcome.

It works best where the outcome can be quantified and expressed numerically. For subjective areas (eg: morality or dignity) it is necessary to go further and look at possible, quantifiable consequences (law suits, loss of earnings, brand deterioration, consumer boycotts, etc).

Example: what is the regret of deciding not to insure a property?

- For a private homeowner it would be major. The annual premium is normally only a small percentage of the property value and the loss (eg: from fire) would be devastating.

- For a company with several properties the annual premiums might be closer to the value of an individual property. Therefore, it might be better not paying the premiums ('self-insuring') and absorbing the loss should it occur. The probability of more than one property burning down is pretty remote.

This principle is now common among large organisations. For example, in fleet insurance the trend is to absorb losses rather than insure (unless the full risk has been laid off by, for instance, outsourcing to a fleet management company).

5. PRIORITISE THE OPTIONS

Having completed the analysis and arrived at a series of options, you must then choose one. Even choosing to do nothing is acceptable as a decision, as long as that course of action is, comparatively speaking, the best option.

Many people find taking a decision difficult, if not impossible, and will try to avoid or defer commitment. This usually arises from self-doubt or an unwillingness to be held responsible. Often an organisation's culture encourages and reinforces such behaviour by employees and will determine the general propensity for people to take responsibility for decisions.

Few organisations measure an individual's ability to take decisions. Moreover, people are frequently put into roles in which decision-making is an integral part and they consequently prove eminently unsuitable.

A manifestation of this is 'blue sky syndrome' where someone arrives at a position of authority and, having been used to referring everything upwards for decisions, looks up and finds no one there, only blue sky. Such people now find themselves faced with the frightening Scylla and Charybdis of management - responsibility and accountability. These and other concepts are explored in the chapter on psychology of decision-making.

5. PRIORITISE THE OPTIONS

OPTION ASSESSMENT MATRIX

Objective	Value of objective	Option 1		Option 2		Option 3		Option 4	
		Probability of objective being met	Probable value	Probability of objective being met	Probable value	Probability of objective being met	Probable value	Probability of objective being met	Probable value
A	5	0.5	2.5	0.2	1.0	0.9	4.5	0.4	2.0
B	4	0.7	2.8	0.7	2.8	0.6	2.4	0.9	3.6
C	3	0.3	0.9	0.8	2.4	0.8	2.4	0.9	2.7
D	2	0.8	1.6	0.6	1.2	0.6	1.2	0.4	0.8
E	1	0.2	0.2	0.4	0.4	0.5	0.5	0.2	0.2
			8		7.8		11		9.3

The value of attaining each objective (A to E) is listed (scoring 1 - 5). The probability of that attainment under each of the four options is then assessed (percentage). By multiplying these two figures you arrive at the probable value of each objective for each of the four options. The overall value per option can then be calculated. In this example option 3 has the best score, followed by 4, 1 and then 2.

A FRAMEWORK FOR DECISION-MAKING

5. PRIORITISE THE OPTIONS

COST vs PRIORITY

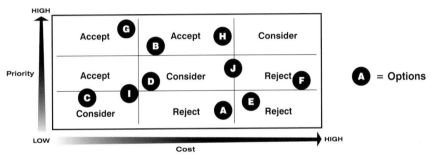

A comparative analysis can yield useful results in those situations where there are several options, many of which can be chosen, but where there is limited capacity for action. *Priority* is contrasted against *cost* to arrive at an acceptable ranking. Those options in the *accept* boxes will be carried out first and then those in the *consider* boxes. Option J clearly needs clarification.

You can then build a plan around the agreed priorities.

5. PRIORITISE THE OPTIONS

PRIORITY GRID

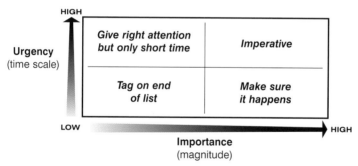

In making decisions it is vital that there is the right balance between urgency (time) and importance (magnitude). Something that is very urgent but is low in importance must be dealt with but without wasting too much time (eg: allocating parking spaces when a new company car park opens the next day). More important issues require greater consideration.

5. PRIORITISE THE OPTIONS

DECISION-MAKING & THE ENVIRONMENT

HIGH	Inspirational
	Judgemental
MEDIUM	Experience
	Consultational
LOW	Routine
Complexity of problem **Uncertainty of environment**	**Appropriate mode of** **decision-making**

You must exercise the appropriate mode of decision-making according to the complexity of the problem and the uncertainty. At the extreme where it is uncertain then, often, inspiration is needed in order to see the optimum decision.

5. PRIORITISE THE OPTIONS

DISCRETION & GOAL ALIGNMENT

Where others are involved in the decision-making process there are two key factors to consider:

- The **discretion** that each party can exercise
- The degree to which their **goals are aligned**

Multi-party decisions are a balance between these two factors.

Where goals are aligned it is much easier to reach agreement than where they are not (eg: in wage negotiations in a cost-cutting environment). In the latter case different processes must be used.

The following grid contrasts the two key factors and identifies the decision-making processes relevant to each.

5. PRIORITISE THE OPTIONS
DISCRETION & GOAL ALIGNMENT

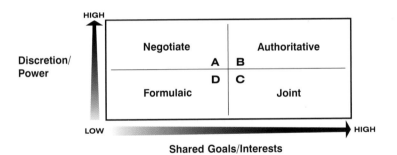

Different processes are used depending on the situation. The grid contrasts the discretion to take decisions against the degree of goal sharing between the parties. See key on next page.

5. PRIORITISE THE OPTIONS

DISCRETION & GOAL ALIGNMENT (KEY)

A   While discretion is high, the goals are not well-aligned. Therefore, negotiation is required to reach a decision (eg: annual pay round).

B   Discretion is exercisable and goals are aligned. An authoritative approach can be taken (eg: a fireman ordering everyone to evacuate a blazing building).

C   Both parties need to work together to make the decision (eg: as in a friendly merger or in compiling a wedding list).

D   Little alignment, no discretion; therefore, use a rule-based formula. For example, with trade contracts there is often a proviso whereby disputes are referred to arbitration, such as when a guarantee is issued and a call made under it. Key here is that the formula **must be agreed in advance** as one party will 'lose'. Another example is a penalty shoot out in a drawn football cup match where the rules have to be clear and agreed up front or the losing party will not be bound by the result.

5. PRIORITISE THE OPTIONS

ETHICAL OR MORAL DECISIONS

Key to ethical or moral decisions is that they are not between right and wrong but, more likely, between right and right depending on your perspective. Ethics or morals ask questions about how we should live or act - and consider the standards against which actions should be judged right or wrong. This is why they are so hard - it is all grey.

One person's decision is another's rejection. This can lead to disputes and disagreements since the basis for decisions is often subjective or emotional. As a result, there is no right or wrong answer because everybody will interpret the outcome according to his or her own stance. Different people will have different perspectives in different situations. Consequently, you will please some people but not others.

Examples:
- Deciding to have a child outside marriage
- Lending to finance the arms trade
- Legalising prostitution
- Legalising 'soft' drugs
- Prohibition in the USA in the 1920s

5. PRIORITISE THE OPTIONS

THERE'S THE RUB...

When it comes down to it you have to take a decision.
Simply ask yourself:

- Do I understand the context?
- Do I know what is wrong and what decision is required?
- Do I know what the options are and the consequences of each?
- Is the argument decisive and incontrovertible?
- What will I regret for each decision?
  (Known in some circles as CISAN -
  Can I Sleep At Night?)

If the answer to all these questions is *yes* -
take the decision!

If not, consider what is stopping you from taking
the decision - and **sort it out.**

6. REVIEW THE DECISION

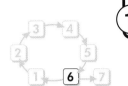

Having taken the decision, at some stage you must review it. The frequency and depth of this will depend on the magnitude of the decision.

There are basically three types of reviews:

- **Periodic reviews** - eg: annual loan reviews, supplier/price reviews, contract expiry reviews, project steering committee meetings
- **Emergency/ad hoc reviews** - where something has changed or new information has emerged which warrants this (eg: a military coup in a country of a major trading partner)
- **Sequential reviews** - where other decisions are based on the outcomes of previous decisions

It's often a good idea for important decisions to be validated by an independent source outside the decision-making body, so the issue can be approached from a different viewpoint. Such a body can ask the 'why' or 'so what' questions that can often add value by challenging some of the assumptions or conclusions. In banks a 'no' decision is often reviewed further up the line to ensure that good opportunities are not lost.

A FRAMEWORK FOR DECISION-MAKING

6. REVIEW THE DECISION
AUTOMATED DECISION-MAKING

Some organisations have automated their decision-making. In credit scoring, for example, you will find:

- **Threshold criteria.** The applicant for credit has to pass all minimum criteria to get through. This is unsophisticated as people who comfortably exceed some criteria may fail on one. A review of this type of assessment may enable better decisions to be made.

- **Weighted scoring.** This is usually a better method as it allows good scores to outweigh poorer scores, and enables more relevant decisions to be made.

Other examples of automated decision-making include:

- **Conjoint analysis.** Very sophisticated, this is used in the car industry, for example, to decide which vehicle features to offer. Consumers are asked to trade off features, one for another, such as a soft-top for a stereo or metallic paint for a wooden fascia. Responses are analysed to develop a model of best preferences. Requiring sophisticated computing programs, the analysis delivers more accurate assessments upon which to base decisions.

- **Expert systems.** Used in insurance underwriting, for example, to assess risk, load premiums and call for further information.

A FRAMEWORK FOR DECISION-MAKING

7. TAKE ACTION

Once a decision has been taken it must be implemented - in other words, something must happen.

A normal sequence would be (high level):

- Make decision
- Tell stakeholders
- Undertake implementation planning
- Commence implementation
- Review
- End implementation

7. TAKE ACTION

PLANNING - GANTT CHART

ID	Task Name	Dur-ation	Start	December	January	February
				30/11 07/12 14/12 21/12 28/12	04/01 11/01 18/01 25/01	01/02 08/02 15/02
1	**commence planning cycle**	60d	**30/11/99**			
2	collect economic data	20d	01/12/99			
3	obtain final sign-off to last year's budget	0d	30/11/99	○ 30/11/99 08:00		
4	analyse	35d	21/01/00			
5	prepare assumptions for planning	25d	02/12/99			
6	obtain sign-off	0d	05/01/00		○ 05/01/00 17:00	
7	circulate to managers	5d	06/01/00			
8	develop budget guidelines	25d	02/12/99			
9	send out to managers	5d	16/02/00			
10	develop corporate targets	35d	29/12/99			

Milestone ○

A GANTT chart is a series of bar charts showing the relative timings of a set of tasks. It will usually show performance time and elapsed time and might well also include resources (man days) and costs.

7. TAKE ACTION

OBTAINING BUY-IN

Where stakeholders have not been involved in the decision-making process, you will need to get buy-in to the decision after it has been made. Handle this extremely carefully or implementation can go very wrong. Example: when accountants Deloitte and Touche tried to merge, it was agreed at global board level. But, at enactment many stakeholders (national partnerships) did not wish to merge and walked away from the deal. Goals were not aligned and discretion of national partnerships was high.

Wherever possible, those involved in implementing a decision should be involved in making the decision. Because:

- Their concerns will have been taken into account
- A deal meeting most of the requirements can be reached
- Problems can be discovered *'ex-ante'* rather than *'ex-post'* when they become crises
- Having been involved in the decision-making it is much harder to walk away from it later
- Key points requiring clarification in subsequent communications can be uncovered
- They can act as 'ambassadors of progress' to sell the deal to others

A FRAMEWORK FOR DECISION-MAKING

7. TAKE ACTION
OBTAINING BUY-IN

The buy-in process must try to get the right message to the right people in the right way.

The method adopted depends on the nature of the stakeholder. The diagram* below shows typical differences in approach.

People	Consulting	Selling
	Delegating	Telling

Task

*After Blake and Moulton

DECISION SUPPORT ANALYSIS

DECISION SUPPORT ANALYSIS

THE THREE STEPS

Analysis is undertaken to assist in decision-making. The three steps are:

1. Carry out the analysis
- Decide what to analyse
- Decide how (methods) and by whom?
- Decide when

2. Collate the analysis
- Pull it all together in sub-sets, logically grouping it
- Formulate conclusions

3. Present the analysis
- Deliver the outputs
  - concisely
  - clearly
  - to different audiences who might have different needs and interests

RULES OF ANALYSIS

Analysis should:
- Model the structure of the problem
- Model the uncertainties
- Model preferences
  - outcomes
  - risk
  - regret
  - benefits/costs, etc
- Adopt a 'what if' approach
- Marshal evidence to support recommendations

These activities can be time-consuming.
Therefore, the exercise **must be cost-effective.**

DECISION SUPPORT ANALYSIS

TYPES OF ANALYSIS

Many types of analysis are used to provide evidence for decisions. Choice depends on what you need to know and the information you need to analyse. Examples include:

- **Decision trees** - to map alternative paths

- **Influence diagrams** - to map what impacts on decisions

- **Scenario planning** - to look at possible future situations and their implications

- **Venn diagrams/matrices** - to display analysis visually

- **Theoretical probability analysis** - often used for education (11-plus, GMAT, CE), market research, voting intentions, environmental risk analysis

SIMPLE DECISION TREES

A decision tree maps the chain of decisions. Consider, for example, the
question of whether to wear a coat or not. The 'map'
with outcomes would look like this:

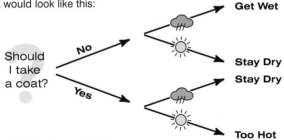

This can be modelled using probabilities,
but there are rules: each option must be linear, the
branches must be mutually exclusive (either it rains or it
doesn't) and all options must be represented. The following example illustrates this…

(59)

SIMPLE DECISION TREES

Should a drug company invest in
developing a new drug, dependent
on getting a patent?

High Sales	0.3
Average Sales	0.5
Low Sales	0.2

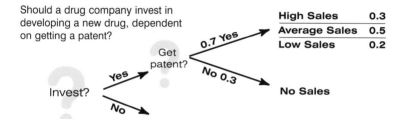

Invest?

Get patent?

Yes

No

0.7 Yes

No 0.3

No Sales

The probabilities of the various outcomes can be calculated by multiplying
along the branches:

High sales probability:	$0.7 \times 0.3 = 0.21$
Average sales probability:	$0.7 \times 0.5 = 0.35$
Low sales probability:	$0.7 \times 0.2 = 0.14$

When translated to revenue and compared with the costs of research and development,
a decision can be made about whether to invest or not.

DECISION TREE ANALYSIS IS ROBUST IF...

- Issues are mutually exclusive – there are no feedback loops connecting the issues
- Issues are collectively exhaustive – detailed issues are the only ones that will significantly affect performance
- Deviations are immaterial – any deviation from these assumptions is a secondary factor that can be ignored
- Answers are additive – aggregating the answers to the detailed issues yields the right answer to the overall issue

In practice, these are taken for granted and rarely checked. Where this is not the case, more complex analysis must be employed. For simple analysis, however, it is sufficient.

DECISION SUPPORT ANALYSIS

INFLUENCE DIAGRAMS

These are ways of analysing decisions diagramatically. In the diagrams below squares represent decisions, circles represent risks, hazards or chances and triangles represent outcomes or consequences. Connecting arrows show the influences.

Let's consider our earlier question *Should I take a coat?* The weather is an uncertainty and if you don't take your coat you could get wet.

Now consider the potential to introduce a new product. The influence diagram would look like the one illustrated here. The revenue and cost are uncertain and, therefore, influence the outcome ('profit' or loss).

DECISION SUPPORT ANALYSIS

INFLUENCE DIAGRAMS

The *new product* model
from the previous page
could be decomposed
further as follows:

Price relates to *revenue* not
cost, but the uncertainty of
sales impacts on both
revenue and *cost* (lower
sales, higher relative fixed
costs). Note, this is not a
flow chart. It represents
decision stages and
influences, whose probability
can be modelled with only a
degree of certainty depending
on the user's assumptions.

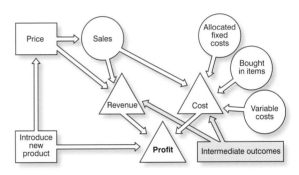

DECISION SUPPORT ANALYSIS

SCENARIO PLANNING

Scenario planning is a technique for analysing how different factors can impact on your business.

- It broadens the thinking from straight-line extrapolations of current situations to consider the wider implications.

- It allows consideration of uncertainties and possibilities.

- It is increasingly being used for planning in uncertainty and to chart 'best course' through several possibilities. It allows you to 'rehearse the future' - to think what might happen and prepare for it.

Four scenarios but several areas of commonality

5 = Common business plan

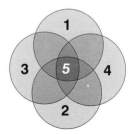

DECISION SUPPORT ANALYSIS

SCENARIO PLANNING

Defined as 'an outline of future development which shows the operation of causes', a scenario:

- Describes a possible future - but is not a prediction
- Challenges the current business model and thinking
- Is engaging, interesting, challenging and credible
- Is logically consistent
- Is broader in scope and considers longer time horizons than a mere forecast

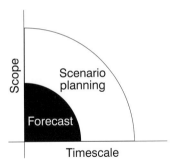

STEPS IN SCENARIO PLANNING

1   Set objectives
2   Identify key issues
3   Classify 'predetermined', 'insignificant' and 'critical' uncertainties
4   Build scenarios
5   Analyse key factors in each; find core elements
6   Examine implications arising from each
7   Identify indicators and monitor

DECISION SUPPORT ANALYSIS

SCENARIO PLANNING
CRITICALITY vs UNCERTAINTY

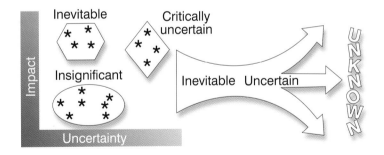

VENN DIAGRAMS

Venn diagrams provide a visual representation of a set of options.

Here, for example, 'A' and 'B' are mutually exclusive - ie: only one or the other can occur but not both (someone dies or lives).

Here 'C' and 'D' demonstrate joint probability - eg: the stock market can go up, the stock can go up or one can and the other does not. The diagram represents the total probability - 'C' plus 'D' plus 'C+D' = 0.6+0.25+0.15 =1.0.
This is also known as Bayes theorem and is used for far more complex analysis.

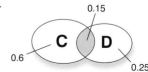

VENN DIAGRAMS

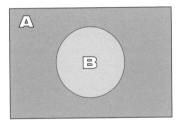

Here 'B' lies wholly within 'A'.
The decision is, therefore, simple.

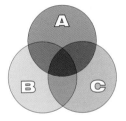

Here 'C', 'B' and 'A' overlap,
showing seven different outcomes
with different probabilities.

MATRICES

A very useful way of setting out the summary issues is by using a matrix. This is very common in presentations where highly complex concepts are reduced to a simple 2 x 2 matrix. The Boston Consulting Group grid is perhaps one of the best known, dividing business units into stars, dogs, problem children and cash cows depending on cashflow and market share.

A grid has many applications. The one below was developed to assist in making lending decisions, contrasting assets of potential debtor and cashflow.

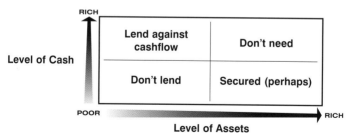

MATRICES

BUSINESS UNIT CATEGORISATION

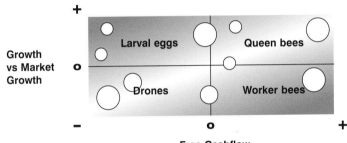

Showing relative growth versus cashflow generation, this allows us to categorise units in terms of value to the organisation. The size of the circles represents the capital allocated. The categories are: value destroyers (drones), value adders (queens), value growers (larva) and steady state (workers).

PROBABILITY – NORMAL DISTRIBUTION

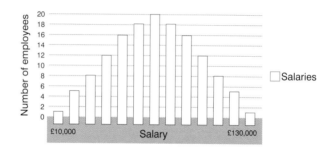

This type of analysis plots the distribution of items against the comparative value (in this case, salaries) and is referred to as a normal distribution or, because of its shape, bell curve. It is the most common of distributions and is used to analyse data in many situations. There are fewer items (salaries in this example) at the top and bottom ends of the scale, as you would expect.

PROBABILITY – OGIVE

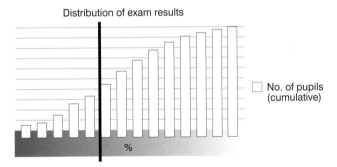

Distribution of exam results

No. of pupils (cumulative)

%

This type of analysis used to be applied in setting the pass marks for exams. A line would be drawn at, say, 40% of the total marks and all above that would be deemed to have passed and all below failed. Thus, each time only a set percentage of candidates passed, negating the debate about easy papers versus difficult papers and the debate about declining standards.

TOOLS FOR DECISION-MAKING

There are numerous decision-making tools around but not all are appropriate to every situation and not every situation has a suitable tool. Tools can be placed in the following categories:

- Expert knowledge systems
- Risk management tools
- Calculation engines
- Simulation models
- 'What if' models

DECISION SUPPORT ANALYSIS

INVESTMENT DECISIONS

Investment decisions are relatively common for anyone involved in almost any aspect of business. They revolve around analysing future cashflows.

One of the main uses is in calculating 'How much should I pay for £x in n years' time?'. To answer the question you calculate:

'What the Net Present Value (NPV) is of £x received in n years' time?'

$$NPV = \sum_{1}^{n} \frac{x}{(1+r/100)^n}$$

Where:
n = Number of periods
r = Interest rate
x = Future sum

Example:

To receive £100 in two years' time, with interest rates at 10%, you would pay
£100 x (1/1.10) x (1/1.10) = £100 x $(1/1.10)^2$ = £82.65.

SEQUENTIAL DECISIONS

Regrettably, life is not so simple that a decision stands alone all of the time. It is far more commonplace to find decisions occurring in sequence, in which each decision is contingent upon the previous decisions taken and will influence subsequent or future decisions. These types of decisions are called dynamic decisions which usually involve asking 'When?' questions as well as 'What?' questions.

In a sequence the final decision 'N' will depend on your time horizon.

Example - export cycle:
Should I take out F/X hedges?
Should I take out an export loan?
Should I take out insurance?
Should I claim interest for late payment?
Should I take court action?

OPTION ANALYSIS: PAY OFF MATRIX

The game of stone, paper and scissors is known to all. Stone grinds scissors, scissors cut paper and paper wraps around stone. There are three outcomes when the game is played by two contestants: player 1 wins, player 2 wins or it is a draw. This can be put in a matrix to analyse the options.

Here is another example. Two people are in jail, pending a court case. There is no evidence unless one of them confesses. The sentence is 10 years. If one confesses and 'shops' his colleague, he receives only three years. The best strategy is not to talk but the most probable outcome is that both confess.

Player 1

Player 2		Stone	Scissors	Paper
	Stone	O	+	− +
	Scissors	− +	O	+ −
	Paper	+	−	O

It demonstrates that no strategy is better than any other, as they all have the same odds (1 in 3) of winning

Prisoner 1

Prisoner 2		Silent	Talks
	Silent	Free	10 yrs 3 yrs
	Talks	3 yrs 10 yrs	3 yrs 3 yrs

DECISION SUPPORT ANALYSIS

WHICH OPTION TO CHOOSE?

It is useful sometimes to contrast efficiency with sustainability which, depending on your requirements, will allow you to choose the best option from among several.

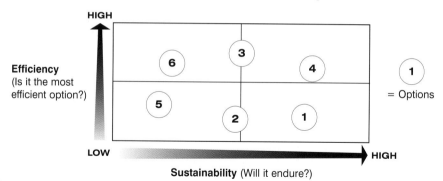

PSYCHOLOGY
OF DECISION-MAKING

GROUPS vs INDIVIDUALS

Much research has focused on the differences between individual and group decision-making.

Many people who have attended supervision or management courses will have played the NASA survival game or a variation of it. Typically, you are placed in a situation and are given some parameters and a restricted number of items that you can take from those available, to assist you in your survival. (Usually, you have crashed in the desert or the jungle, or you are marooned in space or on an island.) You are asked to name in priority order your choice of items that you would take as an individual. This is recorded.

You are then placed into groups and go through the same process of choosing items for survival but now subject to many different views and perspectives. You have to arrive at a consensus of the key items. This is compared with the individuals' lists and discussed. The conclusion is that group members suborn themselves to the will of the group in deciding which items to take. The exercise also gives an opportunity to study behaviours.

PSYCHOLOGY OF DECISION-MAKING

GROUPS vs INDIVIDUALS

In the credit sector studies have compared group lending decisions, made by bank credit committees, with those made by individuals. The results were startling: groups tend to take **more risky** lending decisions than individuals.

While this opposes the belief that entrepreneurs (individuals) rather than corporates engage in risk-taking, the reasons are actually not so far fetched.

Within a group, the feeling of responsibility is more 'collective' but also the risks are argued through from several different views and, therefore, explored in more detail than is the case with individuals.

An entrepreneur typically takes decisions on his or her own without discussing them with others. Some are spectacularly successful (Bill Gates and Microsoft, Richard Branson and Virgin) but others are not.

Successful groups assemble divergent views and use them. Others, however, suffer from **Groupthink**...

GROUPTHINK

Groupthink was identified by the American author Irving Janis. He analysed some of the disastrous decisions in the public sector, such as the Bay of Pigs, Vietnam and Watergate, since these were better documented than decisions made in the private sector. He concluded that the bad decisions were caused by peer pressure to conform, by short-sightedness in looking at the options and by high stress levels which affected judgement.

Peer pressure can force members of a group to conform against their better judgement and not state their view. To avoid this the senior members must not lead the witness and must ensure full and open discussions.

In Japan it is common for juniors to speak first so that they do not contradict a more senior person. Consequently all views are heard.

In law you will often see a judgement given with one judge dissenting (often supported higher up) – an example where groupthink is obviated.

PSYCHOLOGY OF DECISION-MAKING

RACI ANALYSIS

This analysis is very useful when considering exactly who should be involved in decisions and to what extent. It sets out all stakeholders in the decision and then looks at whether they should be:

Responsible for decisions
Accountable for decisions
Consulted about decisions
Informed about decisions

In so doing, it is rare for a stakeholder not to receive the correct attention and, therefore, he or she is less likely to go against the decision.

It is also used to check that stakeholders have indeed been given the required attention. For large projects it is invaluable for managing complex decisions and multifarious stakeholders...

RACI ANALYSIS

		Stakeholders					
		Sponsor	Executives	Shareholders	Suppliers	Council	Unions	Workers
Decisions	1	A	R		C			I
	2							
	3							
	4		A	R			C/I	I
	5							
	6							

R = Responsible **A** = Accountable **C** = Consulted **I** = Informed

PSYCHOLOGY OF DECISION-MAKING

INDIVIDUAL vs GROUP DECISION-MAKING

The major differences in the way that individuals and groups make decisions are contrasted below:

ISSUE	INDIVIDUAL	GROUP
Consensus	Not a problem	Needs to be gained
Divergent views	Not possible	Usually present but must be allowed expression
Wide-ranging experiences	Limited to individual's own	Multi-faceted
Discussion	Does not happen	Needs to be facilitated
Goals	Unity of purpose	Many requiring compromises

THE HERRMANN BRAIN THEORY

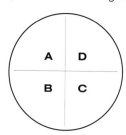

Everyone has a different make-up that influences how they take decisions.
Ned Herrmann's extensive research in this field led to the Herrmann Brain Theory.

There are four parts of the brain. As well as the familiar parts (the cerebral brain) - **Left** (realistic) and **Right** (idealistic) - there are also the less familiar (Limbic) parts - **Top** (thinking) and **Bottom** (doing) [based on the work of Sperry and McLean]. The different parts are combined in different proportions in each individual, as shown in this diagram:

Components of the brain:

A (upper left)   Logical, analytical part
B (lower left)   Form, process, organisational part
C (lower right)   Emotional, feeling part
D (upper right)   Abstract, visioning part

THE HERRMANN BRAIN THEORY

EXAMPLE

The best performing groups have a balance between the four components of the brain, as is the case with the Star Trek officer team:

- Captain Kirk is the visionary leader 'D' and provides the spatial thinking

- Mr Spock is logical 'A' and puts the ideas into logical order and context

- 'Bones' McCoy expresses feelings 'C' and provides the emotions

- 'Scotty' is the pragmatic engineer 'B' and effects the decisions ('I canna break the laws of physics!')

The balance between the characters enables viewers, depending on their own character type, to empathise with one of the officers. This, in part, accounts for the TV programme's success.

It is important, therefore, to understand the type of person you are asking to make a decision. You have to play to his or her style. With groups you have to play to the members. People with similar profiles working together are a dysfunctional group. You will never get the best decisions as members will compete. If, for example, all were 'Ds', they would spend their time generating ideas but take no decisions.

PSYCHOLOGY OF DECISION-MAKING

GROUP DYNAMICS

Rarely are important or critical decisions taken by one person. Usually several people are involved, whether through a hierarchical process (eg: Japanese companies) or in a group, team or committee.

Group dynamics are different from individual dynamics. Members of a group will have group objectives but also their own agenda - their own goals and characteristics.

Each individual's personal goals ...

- Rational
- Political
- Emotional

... must be understood and addressed.

The diagram opposite shows the importance of these three.

GROUP DYNAMICS

What will I get out of this?

What will the impact be on my life?

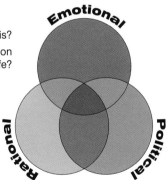

What does it cost and what is the benefit?

Will it work and how long will it take?

Will I look good in the organisation if I support this?

Will it advance my career?

PSYCHOLOGY OF DECISION-MAKING

GROUP DYNAMICS

There are several factors that affect the
efficiency of groups. The balance
between these factors will determine
the group's effectiveness.

In large groups interaction between
members decreases, leadership becomes
more dominant and solutions tend to be
based on politics rather than analysis.

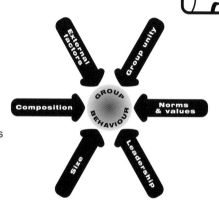

The group devolves into sub-groups around a core. Members on the
fringe contribute little and outliers effectively withdraw.

PSYCHOLOGY OF DECISION-MAKING

GROUP DYNAMICS

To obtain a decision from a group you must understand each of its members and the rational, emotional and political arguments that will convince them.

Each one will ask 'what's in it for me and how can this advance my personal ambition or my status within the group/organisation?' Lack of a satisfactory answer will result in the decision being rejected, either overtly or, more likely, covertly. An overt rejection can at least be dealt with. A covert one is probably more damaging because the decision is opposed tacitly.

You must carry a majority of the group or at least the key decision-makers who will out-vote the rest.

Example: consultants will 'pre-present' their findings to individuals separately and try to deal with their objections in isolation rather than within a plenary forum where damaging arguments could arise.

Studies of juries' behaviour suggest that a majority quickly makes up its mind and the time is spent in persuading the rest to agree/confirm.

SELF-TEST

What are the characteristics of a good decision-maker?

1 _____

2 _____

3 _____

4 _____

5 _____

Compare your answers with the information on the following pages.

CHARACTERISTICS OF DECISION-MAKERS

A good decision-maker requires analysis and problem-solving abilities as well as judgemental abilities.

Analysis and problem-solving

+ Positive
- Takes a step by step approach to finding a root cause
- Understands when they have reached their limitations
- Avoids paralysis of analysis

− Negative
- Cannot distinguish between problems and comments
- Jumps to symptoms rather than the true cause
- Does not learn from experience

PSYCHOLOGY OF DECISION-MAKING

CHARACTERISTICS OF DECISION-MAKERS

Judgemental skills

+ Positive
- Sorts through data and extracts key information
- Focuses on key points
- Provokes and challenges for risks
- Looks at different options
- Changes mind when data changes
- Can take a dispassionate view of the issues
- Facilitates the speed of the decision

– Negative
- Gives equal weighting to all pros and cons
- Only uses partial data
- Relies on face values
- Makes up mind before all data is collected
- Looks for an inappropriate level of detail before deciding
- Does not set priorities for tackling issues
- Procrastinates - refers back or up

PSYCHOLOGY OF DECISION-MAKING

ASSESSING TEAM VIEWS

In multi-variable situations you may need to find out where team members' views lie. Views can be gathered and then plotted to indicate relative positions. If appropriate, responses can be weighted for seniority and/or experience. They can then be plotted on domain diagrams.

Take the example of an organisation deciding on its business goals. It needs to decide whether to go for growth or rationalisation and whether to increase control or move to co-ordination. By plotting each respondent on the domain with a weighting, a quality decision can be made. In the simple, unweighted, example here, the majority of respondents favour growth and co-ordination over control and rationalisation.

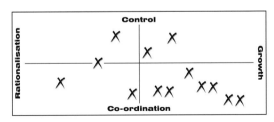

PSYCHOLOGY OF DECISION-MAKING

MEASURING CONSENSUS

The consensus of groups can be measured and plotted to show degree of consensus on options.

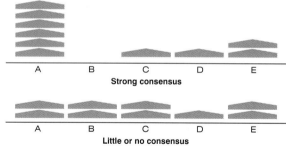

Strong consensus

Little or no consensus

This can tell you which options or strategies to pursue, or to whom pressure needs to be applied in order to obtain a consensus.

COMMUNICATING
A DECISION

COMMUNICATING A DECISION

THE *WHAT* & THE *HOW*

Communication is very important, not only the *what* but also the *how*:

- Decide what you want the people to do/know after the communication
- Define target audiences (eg: executive, staff/union, customers, media, etc)
- Determine the content of message for each audience group
- Identify the most effective and efficient media to use per message per audience group
- Identify barriers to effective communication (organisational and physical)
- Agree best delivery date(s), day, time and situation
- Identify the most effective communicators of the message
- Check if the right message has been heard by the right people at the right time
- Keep at least one step ahead of the target audience's thinking processes
- Prepare for adverse outcomes

COMMUNICATING A DECISION

STRUCTURING YOUR ARGUMENT

To persuade others to support your decision or to lead them into taking the decision that you wish them to take, structure your argument so well that it leads them step by step to the *inescapable, logical* conclusion. This is the same conclusion that you have reached and are now asking them to agree to.

You must lead them to your conclusions without them realising it, by setting out what is common knowledge:

- The situation
- The issue - the complication or what is wrong
- Then the decision that is required

So far they cannot disagree as you are re-stating facts that should be known and understood.

- Then set out the conclusion that is the decision
- Then the supporting evidence
- Faced with such a logical approach most people will readily come to the same conclusions as you and make the decision

The argument must, of course, be constructed logically and contain no flaws.

NOTES

CONCLUSIONS

ESSENTIALS OF DECISION-MAKING

Decision-making is something that happens throughout our day but with different degrees of importance, urgency and consequential outcomes.

The important points are:

- Understand the real objectives
- Know the situation
- Be in control
- Carry out analysis using appropriate tools
- Present findings logically
- Select an option
- Do it!

CONCLUSIONS

BENEFITS OF EFFECTIVE DECISION-MAKING

By following a robust procedure and applying thought and logic to your decision-making process you should be able to make decisions that are:

- **Inclusive** - take into account the interests of all affected parties
- **Defensible** - based on the key points and then weighted and prioritised taking into account the relevant values
- **Optimal** - in both terms of results and in addressing problems
- **Sensible** - and understandable to interested parties
- **Implementable** - differentiate between rational and non-rational as well as rationalised
- **Value-adding** - to the organisation or individual

Success comes from the quality of the decision itself as well as the robustness of implementation or application.

CONCLUSIONS

TIPS

- Once you have finished your deliberations, make the decision quickly - circumstances may change or you may lose momentum.

- Don't sacrifice long-term gain for short-term expediency.

- Understand the difference between **important** and **urgent** - the latter requires a rapid decision, but important decisions may require more protracted analysis. An urgent and important decision needs the right level of analysis to enable the optimal decision to be made.

- Remember, people generally support decisions in which they have participated.

- Do not postpone important but non-urgent decisions - set your own deadlines and do not let them be imposed on you.

- If a decision is no longer appropriate, change it - but in a measured manner, not with a knee-jerk reaction.

- If you need help, get it.

CONCLUSIONS

BUILD THE ARGUMENT

Build the argument until it speaks for itself.

Obvious decision

Context

Issues

Situation

FURTHER READING

Introductory reading:

Pyramid Thinking, Barbara Minto, Pitman, 1990
The Whole Business Brain, Ned Herrmann, McGraw-Hill, 1998

Advanced literature:

Making Hard Decisions, Robert T Clemen, Duxbury Press, 1996
Value Focussed Thinking, Ralph Keeney, Harvard, 1995
Laws of the Game, Eigen & Winkler, Pelican, 1983

About the Author

Neil Russell-Jones

Neil, an MBA, is a management consultant. He is a chartered
banker and a member of the Strategic Planning Society. He
has worked internationally with many organisations, particularly
in the areas of strategy, BPR, change management and
shareholder value. He is a guest lecturer on the City University
Business School's Evening MBA Programme and has lectured
and spoken in many countries. He is also an advisor for The
Prince's Trust. The numerous articles and books written by
him include three other pocketbooks (on marketing, business
planning and managing change), 'Financial Services – 1992'
(Eurostudy) and 'Marketing for Success' and 'Value Pricing',
both published by Kogan Page and, as with 'The Marketing
Pocketbook', written in conjunction with Dr Tony Fletcher.

Contact
You can reach the author on this e-mail: neiljones@neilsweb.fsnet.co.uk

ORDER FORM

Your details

Name _____

Position _____

Company _____

Address _____

_____

_____

Telephone _____

Facsimile _____

E-mail _____

VAT No. (EC companies) _____

Your Order Ref _____

Please send me:

	No. copies
The Decision-making _____ Pocketbook	
The _____ Pocketbook	
The _____ Pocketbook	
The _____ Pocketbook	
The _____ Pocketbook	

Order by Post

MANAGEMENT POCKETBOOKS LTD
LAUREL HOUSE, STATION APPROACH, ALRESFORD,
HAMPSHIRE SO24 9JH UK

Order by Phone, Fax or Internet

Telephone: +44 (0)1962 735573
Facsimile: +44 (0)1962 733637
E-mail: sales@pocketbook.co.uk
Web: www.pocketbook.co.uk

Customers in USA should contact:
Stylus Publishing, LLC, 22883 Quicksilver Drive,
Sterling, VA 20166-2012
Telephone: 703 661 1581 or 800 232 0223
Facsimile: 703 661 1501 E-mail: styluspub@aol.com